Noughts and Crosses

MALORIE BLACKMAN

Level 3

Retold by Karen Holmes

Series Editors: Andy Hopkins and Jocelyn Potter

Pearson Education Limited
Edinburgh Gate, Harlow,
Essex CM20 2JE, England
and Associated Companies throughout the world.

ISBN: 978-1-4082-3162-3

This edition first published by Pearson Education Ltd 2011

4

Original copyright © Oneta Malorie Blackman 2011

Set in 11/14pt Bembo
Printed in China
SWTC/04

For a complete list of the titles available in the Pearson English Readers series, please
visit www.pearsonenglishreaders.com. Alternatively, write to your local Pearson Education
office or to Pearson English Readers Marketing Department, Pearson Education,
Edinburgh Gate, Harlow, Essex CM20 2JE, England.

Contents

Introduction

'I cried because I love you. I'll always love you. But you're a nought and I'm a Cross, and there's no place for us. People will always stand between us. That's why I cried. For everything that we'll never have.'

Sephy Hadley and Callum McGregor are two young people who fall in love. But Sephy is a Cross, the daughter of a government minister, and Callum is a nought. In their world, Crosses and noughts cannot be friends.

Callum's brother, Jude, wants to change the world and joins a group of nought fighters. Because of Jude's activities, Callum becomes a criminal and he loses his sister and his father. Sephy becomes Callum's greatest enemy – but also his great love. Will they ever be together?

Malorie Blackman writes about ordinary people whose lives are destroyed by politicians. One group, the Crosses, control the country and the noughts have nothing. The country is controlled by fear and hate and people are judged by the colour of their skin.

The names of the two groups are important. 'Noughts and Crosses' is a children's game played by two people. When both players are good at the game, neither of them will win. In this book the noughts and Crosses are on different sides. At the end of the story, both groups are losers.

Malorie Blackman has written two more books about the noughts and Crosses, *Knife Edge* and *Checkmate*. Her work is read by young people and adults across the world. She was the first black British writer to sell more than one million books.

Chapter 1 In the Beginning

'Oh, Mrs Hadley,' Meggie McGregor said. 'You're so funny!'

Jasmine Hadley smiled. 'It's good that we're friends.'

Meggie looked across the garden at Callum and Sephy. Her son and her employer's daughter. They were good friends, really good friends. There were no problems for them. Not yet.

'Excuse me, Mrs Hadley.' Sarah Pike, Mrs Hadley's secretary, came out from the house. 'Your husband has just arrived.'

'Kamal is here?' Mrs Hadley was surprised. 'This is his fourth visit in four months. We're popular!'

She stood up and walked towards the house.

'How is Mr Hadley, Sarah?' Meggie asked quietly.

Sarah shook her head. 'He looks angry. I don't know why. I must go back to work. I don't want to get into trouble.'

Meggie looked at the children. Life was simple for them. *I hope their lives will be better than ours*, she thought. *I dream about a different world for Callum and Sephy...*

She turned. Mr Hadley was standing behind her, watching her carefully. 'What are you thinking about?' he asked.

'I was thinking about my son and your daughter. I'd like ...' She stopped, but it was too late.

'What would you like?' Mr Hadley asked quietly.

'I'd like ... them to stay as they are now,' Meggie said quickly. 'Children are so wonderful at this age ...'

Mrs Hadley came out of the house and stood by the door. The strange, worried look on her face made Meggie nervous. Mr Hadley was angry about something – or someone.

'So you had a good time yesterday evening?' Mr Hadley smiled at Meggie.

'Yes. It was quiet ... I ... we stayed at home and watched TV,' she said slowly.

What was happening? Mr Hadley wasn't smiling now. Suddenly he turned to his wife and hit her hard across the face. Then he went back into the house.

Meggie stood up quickly and ran to Mrs Hadley. 'Are you OK?' She put out her hand to touch the side of Mrs Hadley's face.

Mrs Hadley pushed her hand away. 'Leave me alone!' she shouted. 'When I needed your help, you didn't give it.'

'I … what …?' Then Meggie understood. 'You lied to Mr Hadley about last night. About where you were …'

Slowly she lowered her hand. Mrs Hadley turned and angrily walked back into the house. Callum and Sephy were still playing at the end of the garden.

♦

The phone call came that evening.

'It's Sarah Pike here.' The secretary's voice was very quiet. 'I have some bad news for you. Mrs Hadley says … she doesn't want you to work here any more. I'm really sorry.'

Meggie felt cold. Her job was important because her family needed the money.

'Sorry, Meggie,' Sarah said again.

'That's OK. Thanks for telling me. Bye, Sarah.' Meggie put down the phone. 'That's the end of Jude's education,' she said sadly to her husband Ryan. 'How can we pay for it now? Jude must forget about school. He'll have to work.'

'You'll get another job,' Ryan said.

'Not with another Cross family. I won't be able to work for any of Mrs Hadley's friends. We're in trouble.' Meggie stood up. 'I'm going to see her. I've worked for that woman for fourteen years, since she was pregnant with Minerva.'

'I don't think that's a good idea …' Ryan was worried now.

'Ryan, I need to get my job back,' Meggie said. She pulled

on her coat. 'I don't *want* to go to the Hadleys, but I have to.'

Two hours later, Meggie was back at home. And that was the night that her daughter Lynette disappeared.

Chapter 2   Three Years Later

Sephy

My family's private beach was my favourite place in the world. And I was there, on a beautiful August afternoon, with my favourite person. I smiled happily.

'Can I kiss you?' Callum asked suddenly.

I stopped smiling. Kiss me? 'Do you really want to?' I said.

'Yes,' Callum replied.

'OK,' I said. 'But be quick.'

He turned towards me. I moved my head to the left. He moved his head to the left too. I moved my head to the right. He moved his head to the right too.

'How do we do this?' I asked. 'I haven't kissed a boy before. And be quick!'

I kept my eyes open as Callum's head moved closer to mine. It was strange. His skin was soft and his mouth tasted sweet …

I pulled my face away from him. 'No more!' I said.

'It's only strange the first time,' Callum said. 'Let's try again.'

We kissed again – and it was quite nice. I closed my eyes. I felt strange, but not in a bad way. 'That's enough!' I said. 'Have you kissed many other girls?'

'No,' Callum replied.

'Then why did you want to kiss me?'

'We're friends.' Callum smiled. 'Can't you kiss your friends?'

I turned to look at the sea. The sand and sea were so beautiful. My family owned kilometres of the beach.

I looked at Callum. 'What are you thinking?' I asked him.

'About you and me.' Callum looked out over the sea. 'Sephy, do you ever dream about … escaping? Just you and me. Jumping on a boat or a plane and running away?'

'This place isn't so bad, is it?' I asked softly.

'Not for *you*,' Callum replied. 'You're on the inside. I'm not.'

We sat in silence until Callum spoke again. 'Let's start work. What's the lesson today, teacher?'

The sun was too warm and the sea was too blue for schoolwork.

'Callum, you've passed the entrance examination. Why are we still studying?'

'I don't want to give the teachers a reason to throw me out.'

I didn't understand. 'You're in now. The school accepted you.'

'The school is letting me in. It's not *accepting* me.'

I sat up suddenly. 'Maybe you'll be in my class,' I said happily.

'Sephy, I'm fifteen!' Callum said. 'I can't be pleased if they put me − and all the noughts − in a class with twelve- and thirteen-year-olds. With children!'

'I'm nearly fourteen. I'm not a child! And the school explained. You noughts need special lessons …'

'And why is that? Why are we slower in our studies than you?' Callum demanded. 'It's because our schools don't have money and good teachers like your schools. Life's different for us noughts and you Crosses.'

Callum's words hurt me and now I was angry too. 'Us noughts and you Crosses. We're not living in different places with a big wall between us.'

Callum moved closer until his arm touched mine. His skin was warm. He was the only person in the world that I could talk to. But sometimes he seemed so much older and wiser than me. I didn't want things to change between us.

'We must go home,' Callum said. 'Your mum will call the police.'

We left the beach in silence. I looked across the grass towards my parents' house. Seven bedrooms and five living rooms for four people. It was too big, too empty. What did Callum think about it? I liked his house more. People laughed in Callum's house.

'Will I see you tomorrow after school?' I asked.

Callum didn't reply. He was already walking away. Then he started to run – faster and faster.

'PERSEPHONE! INSIDE! NOW!' Mother came running down the steps. She was angry – again. 'Where were you?'

'I was down on the beach.'

She pulled me towards the door. 'Get in the house now. You're not going out again today.'

'Why not?' I asked.

'Stop asking so many questions.'

Callum was the only good thing in my life. I hated meeting him secretly. But Callum was a nought …

♦

Callum

Every time I came back from Sephy's house, I hated my own home. It was small, with three rooms upstairs and two rooms downstairs. We grew vegetables in the garden. The furniture was old and cheap.

'Where were you, Callum?' Mum asked. 'I was worried.'

I sat at the table and looked away from Mum. Dad was busy eating; he never worried about me – or anything. Jude, my seventeen-year-old brother, smiled unpleasantly at me.

'He was with his Cross friend,' he said.

'Callum, were you with her again?' Mum asked angrily.

'No, Mum, I went for a walk.' I turned to my big sister. 'Hi, Lynny,' I said softly.

She smiled at me, then looked down at her hands. I loved Lynette. She looked after me when I was a baby. But now

Lynette couldn't look after herself. She was twenty years old, but she had the mind of a child. Three years ago something changed her. An accident. And suddenly my sister was gone. She didn't go out of the house or talk much. She didn't think much. She was in her own little world.

'Are you ready for school, Callum?' Dad asked. 'I'm so proud of you. My son is going to Heathcroft High School!'

'I still think it's a mistake,' Mum said, looking worried. 'He doesn't need to go to a Cross school. We don't need to mix with them.'

'You'll soon think you're better than us,' Jude said to me. He was always trying to start a fight.

I was excited about school. With a good education I was on my way UP! And then nothing could keep me away from Sephy. Nothing.

♦

Sephy

School tomorrow. The same faces, the same teachers, everything the same. But that wasn't really true. Callum and three other noughts were starting at my school.

I walked out of my room and went quietly down the stairs. I didn't want to see Mother. Three years ago she changed; now she was always unhappy and always drinking. Dad was fun – when he was here. He was always busy. He wanted to be head of the government one day.

Suddenly I stopped. I could hear his angry voice.

'We're letting the blankers into our schools but they're still not happy,' he said.

I stopped, surprised at the word 'blankers'. It was a terrible word for the noughts. It wasn't a word that my father usually used.

Then I heard another voice – Dad had a guest. 'It's the Freedom Fighters. We agree to their demands, then they ask

1 *blanker/dagger.* In this book, these are very rude words for a nought and a Cross. In ordinary English, a blank is an empty space. A dagger is a sharp knife that can kill someone.

for more. They want things to change more quickly.'

'Who's the head of the Freedom Fighters?' Dad asked.

'I don't know, sir. It's taken a long time for them to accept me. They're very careful to keep the name of their boss secret.'

'Find out. That's what I'm paying you for. I'm not losing my place in the government because of them!'

I moved closer to the door. I could see the back of Dad's guest and I was surprised. He was a nought! He had long, fair hair and big brown boots with very pointed toes. Why was he here? Who was he?

I stepped forward again – and then I walked into a table. I didn't make much noise but Dad heard. He looked around and saw me.

'Sephy, go to bed – NOW.' Dad came out of the room and closed the door. 'What did you see?' he demanded. 'What did you hear?' He was really angry.

'Nothing, Dad,' I lied. 'I came down for a drink. I'm thirsty.'

'Go and get one – quickly.'

He watched me go into the kitchen and pour a glass of water. Then I went back upstairs.

'Princess, wait …' Dad called me back and spoke more softly. 'I'm sorry I was angry. I've had a difficult day.'

'That's OK,' I whispered.

I walked up the stairs. And Dad stood and watched me.

♦

Callum

That evening Mum came into my room and sat on my bed.

'I'm proud that you're going to Heathcroft School,' she said. 'I just want you to be happy. I don't want you to get hurt.' She tried to smile. 'Some of the Crosses aren't happy about noughts going to their schools. If they make trouble, don't fight with them. Don't give them a reason to throw you out of the school.'

'Don't worry,' I said. 'I passed the exam and now I'm going to stay there.'

We went downstairs together. Lynette and Dad were sitting on the sofa. Jude was looking at a map.

I sat next to my sister.

'Are you OK?' That strange look was back in her eyes. *Please Lynette*, I thought. *Not tonight ... not now ...*

'Why am I here?' Her grey eyes looked worried. 'I don't belong here. I'm a Cross.'

'What are you talking about?' Jude demanded. 'You're a nought. Look at your skin. You're as white as I am. Whiter.'

'Jude, stop,' Dad said quickly.

'No, I'm tired of this. Lynette thinks she's a Cross. She's crazy. And Callum thinks he's better than us. As good as the Crosses.'

I stood up. I was ready for a fight, but Dad stopped us.

'Look at my skin,' Lynette said. 'It's a beautiful colour. So dark and wonderful. I'm so lucky that I'm a Cross.' She looked happily down at her hands – her pale, white hands. Then she looked at me and smiled. I smiled back at her.

Chapter 3 First Day at School

Sephy

When I arrived, there was a crowd of adults and Heathcroft pupils outside my school. They were shouting, 'NO BLANKERS IN OUR SCHOOL! NO BLANKERS IN OUR SCHOOL!' Police officers were standing near Callum and three other noughts at the school entrance. I pushed my way through the crowd towards them.

'Callum! CALLUM!' I called.

I saw my sister Minnie. She was shouting loudly too: 'NO BLANKERS IN OUR SCHOOL!' The angry crowd pushed forward again. Suddenly Callum's head disappeared.

'One of them is hurt!' someone shouted.

Callum ... It wasn't Callum, was it?

The police officers were pushed to the ground as people ran forward. Then I saw Callum on his knees next to a nought girl. There was blood on her face and her eyes were closed.

'Stop it! Just stop it!' I shouted. 'YOU'RE ACTING LIKE ANIMALS. WORSE THAN ANIMALS – LIKE BLANKERS!'

The crowd slowly became quiet. I looked down at Callum. There was a strange look on his face.

Callum, not you. I called those other people blankers, not you. I wanted them to stop ...

Later we sat together on the beach. It was a beautiful evening at the end of a terrible day.

'I'm sorry,' I said to Callum. 'It's just a word, Callum.'

'I know you're sorry. But Sephy, you used that word.'

I started to cry. 'It was a mistake ... I was trying to help. Please don't hate me. You're my best friend.'

'Promise me that you'll never use that word again.'

It was just a word. A word that Dad used. But it was a word that hurt my best friend. A word that was now hurting me.

'I promise.' I moved closer to him and put my head on his shoulder. He didn't move away, but he didn't put his arm around me. All this trouble between us because of one word.

The sun started to go down, turning the sky pink and orange.

'We can still be together sometimes, but don't talk to me in school,' Callum said.

I was surprised. 'Why?'

'I don't want you to lose your friends because of me.'

'But you're my friend too.'

'I'm not your friend at school.' Callum stood up. 'I'm going home now. Are you coming?'

'Don't worry about me,' I said. 'I'll stay here a bit longer.' I gave him his jacket and he walked away. He didn't look back.

♦

Callum

'Are you OK, son?' Dad asked. 'I went to Heathcroft when I heard about the trouble. The police stopped me so I couldn't get in. So how was school? How were your lessons?'

'I was OK, Dad,' I lied. School was hard. The teachers didn't speak to us, and the Crosses threw our books onto the floor. 'It was fine.'

'You were on TV,' Jude said. 'Your "friend" was too. Everyone heard her say …'

'It was a mistake,' I said.

'Miss Sephy is growing up like her mother,' Mum said.

'You and Sephy's mum were friends, remember?' I said.

Mum was Minerva's and Sephy's nurse when they were children. I grew up with Sephy. One week Mum and Mrs Hadley were best friends and the next week we weren't welcome at the Hadley house. That was three years ago.

The news came on the TV. The first report was about the Freedom Fighters. Sephy's father, Kamal Hadley, was speaking. 'There is no hiding place for noughts who are in the Freedom Fighters. Reports suggest that the car bomb outside the International Business Centre last month was their work. We will find and punish them. Guilty noughts will die.'

Then Jude surprised me. 'Long live the Freedom Fighters!' he shouted. Dad smiled at him. Did they belong to the group? I didn't mind, but why didn't they tell me?

Then Heathcroft School was on TV. The camera showed Sephy, shouting at the crowd. 'Persephone Hadley, daughter of government minister Kamal Hadley, helped to stop the trouble …' And then, again, she shouted out those words.

10

I stood up. 'I'm going to my room.'

I closed the door behind me but I could hear Jude's voice. 'They're all the same. Crosses and noughts will never be friends. Callum's stupid. That Cross girl doesn't really like him.'

'*We* know that,' Dad said. 'But *he* doesn't.'

I went upstairs. Maybe my family was right and I was wrong.

♦

Sephy

Callum and the other noughts were the last pupils to come into the history lesson. I smiled at Callum and pointed at the seat next to me. Callum looked away and sat next to another nought.

At the end of the lesson, I went to have lunch. Callum and the other noughts were sitting together at a table. I walked towards them. I wanted to show everyone that Callum was my friend.

'Can I sit with you?' I asked.

They looked surprised when I sat down.

'What are you doing?' Callum asked angrily.

'Eating my lunch,' I replied. I smiled at the other three noughts. 'Hi, I'm Sephy Hadley.' The nought girl next to me had a brown plaster on her face. It was very dark against her white skin. I held out my hand. 'Welcome to Heathcroft.'

She looked at my hand, surprised. Then she took it and shook it slowly. 'I'm Shania,' she said quietly.

'How's your head?' I asked. I pointed at the plaster. 'That plaster is the wrong colour for you.'

'The shops don't sell pink plasters. Only dark brown ones,' Shania said.

She was right. Plasters were the colour of Crosses' skin, not the noughts' skin.

'Sephy, what are you doing?' said one of the teachers, Mrs Bawden. 'Go back to your own table – immediately.'

What table? I didn't have a table. And then I understood.

I looked at Callum but he turned away from me. He and the other noughts couldn't look at me.

'I'm sitting with my friend Callum,' I whispered. Everyone in the dining-room was looking at me.

Mrs Bawden pulled me out of my chair. 'Persephone Hadley, come with me!' She started to push me across the room.

I stopped fighting Mrs Bawden and followed her.

♦

Callum

That evening, I sat on the beach as the sun went down. The Crosses didn't want us in their schools. They didn't want to give us a good education or good jobs. We were noughts … Nothing. Zero.

I sat there for a long time before I saw Sephy. She was standing on the beach, watching me. Then she turned away.

'Sephy, wait.' I ran after her and took her arm. 'Aren't you going to stay?'

'No. I don't stay where I'm not wanted.'

'Stop it, Sephy!' I said.

'Stop what?' she shouted angrily. 'You're no different to the others. "Crosses and noughts can't be seen together. Crosses and noughts can't live in the same world."'

'That's not true. You know that I don't believe that.'

'Do I? You'll only talk to me if nobody is watching.'

This time, when she walked away I didn't stop her.

Chapter 4 The Fight

Sephy

Everything was wrong. People at school were pointing at me and whispering about me. And I didn't want to see Callum. But I couldn't sit in the school toilet all day.

I stood up and opened the door. Lola, Joanne and Dionne from the class above mine pushed me back inside.

'We heard about yesterday,' Joanne said. 'You sat on the blankers' table in the dining-room.'

'Why do you spend time with the blankers?' Dionne demanded. 'They smell bad and they eat strange food. And they don't wash.'

'That's not true!' I said. 'Callum washes every day and he doesn't smell. None of the noughts smell. Why do you hate them?'

'They start trouble,' Lola said. 'They all belong to the Freedom Fighters. They're stupid. They have blank, white faces and blank minds. Blank, blank, blank. That's why we're better than them.' She hit me across the face.

Were they serious? 'Noughts are people, like us,' I said. 'You're the stupid one …'

Lola hit me across the face again, but this time I fought back. I hit Lola in the stomach but she and Joanne took hold of my arms.

Dionne looked at me. She was the best fighter in the school. She smiled slowly. 'Blanker-lover,' she said. Then she really hurt me.

◆

Callum

It was the end of another bad day at school.

'Callum, wait.' Shania was running towards me. 'Have you heard about Sephy? Somebody attacked her in the school toilets.' Shania was excited, pleased. 'I'm not surprised. She thinks she's better than us. She probably washed her hand after she touched mine.'

I ran to the Hadleys' house and knocked loudly on the door.

'Yes?' Sarah Pike opened the door and looked at me.

'I want to see Sephy – please.'

'She can't see anyone.' Sarah tried to shut the door in my

face. I put my foot between the door and the wall.

'I want to see Sephy. Is she OK?'

'She's badly hurt and very frightened. The doctor wants her to stay at home until the end of the week.'

'Who is it, Sarah?' Mrs Hadley stopped on the stairs when she saw me. 'You're the McGregor boy, aren't you? What do you want?'

'I want to see Sephy, please.'

'My daughter was attacked because she sat at your lunch table yesterday. You turned away from her. Is that true?'

'You don't understand,' I said angrily. 'If she sits with us, it makes her friends angry. I didn't want more trouble.'

'I don't believe you,' Mrs Hadley said. 'Sarah, make sure this … boy leaves. I don't want him near my house again.'

'I'm sorry.' Sarah pushed my foot away and closed the door.

Nobody understood. Nobody.

I didn't see Sephy for five days. Then, when she came into the classroom she didn't look at me. At the end of the lesson I stopped her. 'Sephy, wait. Are you OK now?'

She spoke very quietly. 'Yes, thank you.'

'I was worried about you.'

'I don't believe you. You didn't come to see me. You didn't send me a card.'

'I came to see you every day!' I said. 'Your mother kept me away from you. I stood outside the gates of your house every afternoon. Ask your mother … no, ask her secretary.'

'You came to see me?'

'Every day. Sephy, nothing can keep me away from you.'

She looked at me. 'I have to go now,' she said. But she believed me.

When I arrived home, Lynette was shouting at Jude. Dad was standing between them. Mum wasn't there. There was blood on Jude's mouth.

'You're rude and uneducated!' Lynette screamed at him.

'You think you're too good for us,' Jude said angrily. 'Well, you're not. When the daggers look at you, they see a *white* person.'

'I'm *not* white! I'm *brown*. Look at my dark skin.'

Jude pulled her to the mirror on the wall. 'See?' he shouted. 'We're both white. Stop thinking that you're better than me!' He pushed her away and she fell against the mirror.

'Dad, do something,' I shouted at him.

'Jude, stop!' said Dad.

'Someone has to tell her she's a blank. *You* won't – you're too weak. Mum won't say anything because Lynette is her favourite child. And Callum is only interested in his dagger friend Persephone.'

'You think you're always right,' I said. 'I hate you.'

Jude turned and ran towards me. He hit me hard in the stomach and I fell to the ground. Dad pulled him away and hit him across the face. We all stopped moving. Dad never hit us.

He spoke more quietly. 'You don't know what happened to your sister. Don't judge her.'

'W-what happened to her?' Jude asked. He was touching the side of his face. Suddenly he was a small boy again.

'Three years ago, your mum lost her job. We didn't have any money and you left school. At the same time, three or four nought men attacked Lynette and her boyfriend, Jed. They almost killed him and she was in hospital for more than two weeks.'

'I didn't know …' Jude said slowly. This was news to me too. Who was Jed? 'You said ...'

'She didn't want us to tell you. She was attacked because her boyfriend was a Cross. And we didn't know about him. She was too frightened to tell us. The attack destroyed her mind … She's still hurting. So don't fight with her. Do you understand? DO YOU UNDERSTAND?'

'Yes,' Jude said.

I looked at Lynette, my sister Lynette.

'Where's Jed, Daddy?' she whispered.

'Jed? Jed went away a long time ago,' Dad said softly.

Lynette looked worried again. 'Where am I?' she asked.

'At home,' Dad said. 'You're safe now.'

'Lynette, I didn't know.' Jude held out a hand to her, but she pushed it away.

'Keep your hands away from me,' she said angrily.

Jude pulled his hand away from her. 'My nought hands, you mean. Your hands are the same as mine,' he said. 'The same as theirs.'

Lynette turned and ran up to her room.

Chapter 5   A Death in the Family

Sephy

'Don't be so unkind, Kamal,' Mother said. 'It makes me so unhappy.'

'Then go and drink another few bottles of wine,' Dad shouted. 'You're good at that.'

Minnie and I were sitting on the stairs, listening. Mother and Dad were in the family room, fighting.

'Why are you so unpleasant to me?' Mother asked. 'I'm a good wife to you, a good mother to our children.'

'Oh, yes,' Dad agreed angrily. 'You've been an excellent mother to *all* my children.'

I didn't understand. What did Dad mean?

'Did you really want to bring that child into our house?' Mother shouted. 'Did you really think I could agree to that?'

'Oh, no! Of course the great Jasmine Adeyebe-Hadley couldn't have my son in her house! Of course I understood.'

Dad had a son? Minnie and I had a brother? I turned to my sister. She was looking at me. We had a brother …

'I was wrong. But I was hurt. I didn't know you had another child when we married.' Mother started to cry. 'Kamal, maybe we can start again. You and me. Let's go away somewhere together and …'

'Oh, Jasmine, don't be stupid,' Dad said. 'Our marriage is a joke. Look at you. You drink too much – you're a boring drunk.'

'I helped you to become a government minister,' Mother said. Her voice was shaking. 'And now you want to leave me for that woman …'

'Her name is Grace,' Dad said angrily. 'You and the children will get everything you need. And I want to see the girls. I love them.'

I heard him walk out and close the door noisily. I ran upstairs to my bedroom. I didn't cry. Dad had another woman and was leaving home. And I had an older brother. Everything in my life was a lie.

Later that night, I went to my sister's room. She was sitting on her bed with tears in her eyes. 'We have a brother!' I said.

'He's not our brother. He's just our dad's son.' Minnie stood up and walked over to the window.

I sat down on a chair. 'How do we find him?'

'Are you crazy? We're not going to find him.' Minnie said angrily. 'I learned about him three years ago. I didn't want to meet him then and I don't want to meet him now.'

'Three years ago!' I shouted. 'Why didn't you tell me?'

'It's not important. Dad had a son before he met Mother. That's all I want to know.'

'Minnie, don't you want to know our brother's name?'

'Stop calling him our brother. And no, I don't.'

'Well, I do. I'm going to ask Dad and …'

Minnie ran across the room and pulled me off my chair.

'You will not! Mother's already unhappy about Dad's son. Don't make it worse.'

'Is that why she's unhappy? Because of Dad's son?'

'That's part of the reason. Also, there was another man …'

'Mother? Mother had a lover?'

'She wanted Dad to notice her and to spend more time with her,' Minnie said. 'But it didn't work. Then she felt even more alone. She hasn't got any real friends.'

'She's strange. One minute she's nice to people, then she's unpleasant to them.'

'She's lonely,' said Minnie.

I didn't understand my family. Mother was unhappy and her drinking was getting worse. Dad wanted to leave her because he loved another woman. Minnie was always angry and sad. And I couldn't help any of them.

Later that night, I was watching TV when Minnie ran into my room. 'Sephy, phone for a doctor. Quickly!'

I followed her into Mother's bedroom. Mother was lying on the floor, a medicine bottle at her side. Minnie sat down next to her and held her head. 'A doctor. Now!' she screamed.

I ran to the phone. Mother tried to kill herself …

♦

Callum

We were eating dinner and nobody was speaking. Lynny kept her head down. Jude was still angry. Dad's face was sad.

Mum put down her knife and fork. 'What's wrong?' she demanded.

Lynny stood up. 'I'm going for a walk. I'll be back soon.'

'Do you want me to come with you?' I asked.

'No,' she said. She ran upstairs. A few minutes later she came down again. 'I'll see you later. Goodbye, everyone.' She smiled, the saddest smile. Then she shut the door and was gone.

Three hours later, she was still not home. Mum was angry with Dad. 'Jude and Lynette were fighting and you didn't stop them? You're a weak man! And where is my daughter now?'

'Dad tried to stop us,' Jude said.

'Be quiet. I'm tired of listening to you. You think you're always right. You're unpleasant to your sister –'

Suddenly there was a knock at the door. Jude opened it. Two police officers were standing outside. One was tall and thin, the other was short and fat. They were both Crosses, of course.

'Mr McGregor?' The tall officer looked around the room. Dad stood up slowly.

'Lynette ...' Mum whispered.

'I'm Officer Collins and this is Officer Darkeagle. I'm afraid we have some bad news.'

'What's happened?' Dad asked quietly.

'You have a daughter called Lynette McGregor?' Officer Collins asked. 'I'm very sorry, sir. There was an accident ... She walked in front of a bus. She was killed immediately.'

'NO!' Mum screamed and went down on her knees. Dad ran to her side and put his arms around her. She didn't speak and she didn't cry. She didn't make another sound.

Officer Collins stepped forward and gave Dad a card. 'This is my number. If you need anything, phone me. I'm very sorry.'

The door shut quietly behind them. Mum opened her eyes slowly. A tear ran down her face.

I went up to my room and lay on the bed. My sister was dead. Why couldn't I cry? I turned on my side and felt something under the bedcover, an envelope. *Callum* was written on it in my sister's small writing.

'Lynny?' I whispered. I picked up the letter and opened it.
Dear Callum,

It's hard to write this letter. I'm tired and I want to die. I don't

want to live in a world where I'm a nought, a nothing. I hope you and Sephy have better luck than Jed and me. Be strong for both of us.
All my love, Lynette

For the first time in my life I hated my sister. Hated her. She gave up her life. I could never do that. Never.

A week after Lynette's 'accident', our house was full of people – friends, family, neighbours, strangers – who wanted to say goodbye to her. There was a lot of noise and I wanted to escape. Jude was with his friends, drinking. He never smiled now. Dad was standing in a corner with two other men. One of them had dark brown hair and dark skin. Maybe he was half nought, half Cross – lucky man.

The man pressed something into Dad's hand and Dad put it quickly in his jacket pocket. Mum came in, looked angrily at the two men, then made her way purposefully towards them.

But suddenly the room was silent. Nobody spoke or moved. I turned.

Sephy … Why was she here? Was she crazy? She walked past me to my mum and dad.

'Mr and Mrs McGregor, I'm so sorry about Lynette …' Her voice was very quiet. 'I wanted to say …'

Mum was the first to speak. She stepped forward. 'Thank you. Can I get you a drink?'

Sephy looked around. People were looking at her, and their faces were unfriendly. 'No, I don't think I should stay.'

Dad was alone in the corner of the room. The two men weren't there. He looked at Sephy angrily. 'Hello, Miss Hadley,' he said.

'I'll go.'

'Sephy …' I stepped forward but Jude pushed me away.

'Yes, go!' he said angrily. 'We don't want you here.'

'Jude, be quiet,' Mum told him.

'You and the other daggers bring us trouble.' He pushed Sephy hard on her shoulder. Noughts never pushed Crosses.

'Go away,' he said.

Sephy looked around for me. 'But I haven't done anything...' she said.

I tried to step forward but a woman stopped me. 'Leave her. Noughts don't mix with Crosses, boy,' she whispered to me.

Sephy ran out of the room. There were tears in her eyes.

'That was wrong, Jude,' Mum said.

'No, it wasn't,' Dad said angrily. 'We didn't want her here.'

Mum looked at him, surprised. Dad was never angry with anyone.

'Meggie, it's time to do something,' he said. His voice frightened me.

Chapter 6   The Bomb

Callum

It was more than three months after Lynette's death. Jude and Dad were sitting at the table, looking at a map. Mum was out, walking. Suddenly Dad stood up. 'Come with me, Jude,' he said.

'Where are you going, Dad?' I asked.

'To a meeting.'

'What meeting? Can I come?'

'No, you're too young,' said Dad. He put on his coat.

What were they doing? My house was full of secrets. Mum was always sad and she never talked to us. I missed Lynette.

'I want to come with you,' I said. 'If Jude belongs to the Freedom Fighters, I can join too.'

'What?' Dad turned angrily to Jude. 'Jude, you stupid boy! How does he know about the Fighters?'

'I didn't say anything, Dad, I promise,' Jude said.

'Jude didn't tell me.' I said. 'I guessed.'

'You can't come. We're going to a meeting and you're too

young. If somebody sees you there, you'll be in trouble. It will end your education. Do you want that?' Dad asked.

'There's nothing for me at Heathcroft. The other noughts – Colin and Shania – have already gone. I want to leave.'

'You will *not* leave,' Dad shouted angrily. 'You'll stay at school until you're eighteen. Then you'll go to university. Do you understand?' He went to the door.

'And don't tell your dagger friend about the Freedom Fighters,' Jude whispered to me. 'If you do, the Crosses will hang us.'

The weeks passed slowly until, one Saturday, it was five months and eighteen days after Lynette's death. Nobody knew the true story about her death except me. I wanted to tell someone. I wanted to tell Sephy …

I spoke to Sephy on the phone. She was going shopping with her mother. Sephy hated shopping.

'Maybe we can meet later,' I said.

'I'll see you at the café,' Sephy said.

'If I miss you, I'll meet you at the beach at about six o'clock,' I said.

After lunch, I picked up my jacket and went towards the door.

'Where are you going?' Mum asked.

'The shopping centre.'

Jude jumped up. 'No you're not. Not today,' he said nervously.

'Why can't I go?' I asked my brother. 'What's happening there?'

I turned to Mum. She was looking at Jude with fear in her eyes.

'Don't go there, Callum,' Jude told me.

'But …' Then I understood. The Freedom Fighters were planning something at the Dundale Shopping Centre. Jude knew about it. And then I remembered.

'Sephy's at the shopping centre!' I cried.

'Callum …' Jude began.

I didn't wait to hear his words. I ran out of the house towards the shopping centre.

♦

Sephy

Mother went back to the car park with her shopping, so I went to the café. I was happy to get away from her.

'Sephy! You must leave here.'

'Callum!' I said happily. 'Where did you come from?'

'It's not important. You have to leave – NOW!'

I looked at him. He was frightened, really frightened. He pulled me out of my seat towards the café door.

'Is that boy troubling you?' a stranger asked me.

'No! No, he's a friend of mine,' I said. 'He wants to show me something …'

Then we were running to the shopping centre exit. Suddenly everyone was shouting and running with us. Callum was pulling me after him.

Then there was a loud noise and I was thrown to the ground. I was lying outside, on my face. I looked back at the shopping centre and saw smoke. I heard people screaming, then the sound of police cars.

'Are you OK?' Callum asked. 'You're not hurt?'

'Y-you knew …' I shook my head. No, that was silly. He couldn't know about the bomb … 'Mother! Oh no!' I ran quickly across the street towards the car park. On the way, I turned to look back at Callum. He was gone.

♦

Callum

When I walked into the house, Mum was waiting for me. 'Where were you?' she asked. 'Where's Jude? Isn't he with you?'

'No. Isn't he here?' I said, closing the door. Suddenly I was very tired.

I switched on the television. A news reporter was speaking, his face very serious. 'Thirty minutes ago, there was a bomb attack at the Dundale Shopping Centre. Seven people died and many more are badly hurt. The nought group, the Freedom Fighters, sent a message about the bomb only five minutes before the attack.'

'That's not true,' Jude said. He was standing behind us now with Dad. On the TV, there were pictures of people on the ground, broken windows, blood.

Mum turned to Dad, white-faced. 'Ryan, did you or Jude place that bomb at the shopping centre? Promise me it wasn't you.'

'Don't ask questions!' Dad said angrily. He never spoke to Mum like that.

Mum looked at him, then turned to Jude. 'Jude, did you put that bomb in the shopping centre? NO! Don't look at your father. I asked you a question – now answer it.'

Jude looked from Mum to Dad, then he spoke. 'We were ordered to, Mum. A few of us placed the bomb last night. But the Fighters planned to send a message to the police an hour before the attack. Dad told us that …'

'You murdered all those people …' Mum whispered. Her body was shaking. Dad touched her arm. She turned and hit him hard across the face.

'You lying, murdering … You promised me. You were only helping to *plan* an attack. You promised me! And now Jude is part of it.'

'I'm sorry …' Dad began.

'Sorry? Sorry? Tell that to the families of those dead people,' Mum shouted at him.

Dad stood up straight. His eyes were angry again. 'Now the Crosses know that we're serious.'

'I have nothing more to say to you,' Mum said and left the room.

The next day, she told Dad. 'I want you to leave before tomorrow morning. It's too late for you and me, but it's not too late for Jude. I can still save him.'

'If Dad leaves, then I'll leave too,' Jude said.

'No, you won't.' Mum and Dad spoke together.

'I won't leave the Freedom Fighters,' Jude said. 'For the first time in my life I'm doing something useful.'

'Then you can both leave this house tomorrow,' Mum said coldly. 'And I'll protect Callum. I'll save one of my children.'

The police came later that night. They broke down the front door. There was a scream, the sound of running feet on the stairs.

'Jude? Jude?' I shouted. Was he still asleep?

'DOWN! GET DOWN!' a voice screamed at me. There were more voices, then someone pushed me. My face hit the hard floor and I bit my tongue. They hurt me as they pulled my arms behind my body.

'JUDE! MUM! DAD!' I called. They pulled me out of the house, into the cold night air. As I was pushed into a car, I heard Mum. She was crying.

'MUM!' I called. I couldn't see her. My hands were tied behind my back and every part of my body hurt.

At the police station, two officers questioned me. 'Tell us about your brother. When did he join the Freedom Fighters?'

'He didn't.'

'When did your mother join?'

'She didn't.'

'Was the Dundale bomb your brother's or your father's idea?'

Question after question. They didn't stop for hours. Where were Mum and Dad and Jude? What were they doing?

Finally they let Mum in to see me. 'Callum? Are you OK? Did they hurt you?'

'Where's Dad? Where's Jude?' I asked.

'They are questioning your dad,' Mum said quietly. 'I don't know where Jude is. He wasn't in the house.'

'What do they want? Why are they asking about Jude?'

'They found an empty drink can near to the Dundale bomb. They say his fingerprints are on it. W-when they catch him, he'll … he'll hang.'

'If they only want Jude, why are they questioning Dad?'

Mum was crying. 'I don't know.'

The door opened and an officer came in. 'You can leave now,' he said.

'Where's my husband?' Mum asked.

'We're keeping him.'

'Why?' Mum asked angrily. 'He's done nothing wrong. I want to see him!'

The officer couldn't help us. 'Only his lawyer can see him now. He's murdered seven people.'

The next day, we went back to the police station. Dad's lawyer, Mr Stanhope, was in another room, talking to him. When he came out to us, he looked very serious. 'Come with me, please,' he said.

We followed him. A police officer opened one of the heavy doors of a police cell and Mum ran to Dad. 'Ryan, what's happening?' she whispered. 'Are you OK? You're not hurt …?'

Dad turned and put his arms around me. I wanted him to hold me because I was so frightened. Why was he still here?

'Mr McGregor, please repeat your story,' Mr Stanhope said.

'That's not important,' Dad said. 'Where's Jude? Have the police freed him? Is he safe?'

'Jude?' Mum said. 'The police didn't catch him. He wasn't in the house. I don't know where he is.'

Suddenly Dad was so angry that I stepped away from him, afraid. 'But the police have him! They told me!' he shouted.

Then he turned away from Mum and me. 'No!'

'Ryan, w-what did you do?' Mum whispered.

'I signed a confession that I'm the Dundale bomber. I wanted to save Jude. They found his fingerprints on a can near the bomb. They found the same fingerprints on part of the bomb. The police want to hang Jude and put you and Callum in prison. Now they have my confession, they won't take you.'

'Did you kill those people?' Mum asked. 'Did you put that bomb in the shopping centre?'

Dad looked straight at Mum. 'No.'

Then Dad spoke loudly so the police officers outside the room could hear him. 'I brought the can from home. Jude probably took it out of the fridge and put it back again. And the bomb … I kept parts of it in the house. Jude probably touched those too. He didn't know what they were. I'm guilty, not Jude.'

'Ryan …' Mum started to cry. 'They'll hang you …'

Dad lowered his voice. 'Jude won't die, and you and Callum won't go to prison. Keep Jude away from the daggers. They mustn't find him.' He smiled sadly.

Chapter 7 The Execution

Sephy

Of course Callum's dad wasn't the bomber. I wanted to help him – but how?

Everything was going wrong. Callum and his mother were hiding somewhere with relatives. Callum wasn't at school. The teachers didn't want the son of a murderer at Heathcroft.

Every night I watched Mr McGregor's trial on the television news. One night someone burned and destroyed Callum's house. I cried and cried. I wanted to see him but I didn't have his new address. I went to the beach sometimes but he was never there.

♦

Callum

The trial started. Dad had another lawyer in court, Kelani Adams. She was one of the best lawyers in the country. She was also a Cross.

'We can't pay for her,' Mum said to Mr Stanhope. 'She's too expensive.'

'Someone is paying her bills,' Mr Stanhope said. 'I received a cheque and an unsigned letter. Someone wants to help you.'

Mum was a proud woman and she didn't want to accept money from a stranger. She looked at me. 'Callum? What shall we do?'

'We have to help Dad,' I said.

'Ok,' Mum said. 'If it helps my husband, we'll take the money.'

On the first day of the trial I sat in the court and watched Dad. He looked sad.

The court officer stood up and said, 'Ryan Callum McGregor, are you guilty or not guilty of murder?'

Dad looked up at Mum and me. He was silent for a long time, then he surprised everyone.

'Not guilty!' he said. His voice was loud and strong.

The lawyers questioned me during the trial, then they questioned Sephy. The police had film of me pulling Sephy out of the café in the Dundale Shopping Centre.

'You knew about the bomb!' the police lawyer said to me.

'No!'

'Why did you take her out of the café?'

'I wanted to show her something ...'

The lawyer didn't believe me, but Sephy told the same story to the court, and the stranger from the café also remembered my words.

It seemed to me that other people controlled every part of my life. I felt helpless. At night I often dreamed that I was a prisoner in a box. I pushed at the sides until my hands were bloody. But there was no way out. In my dream I could never escape. So I stopped fighting and waited to die.

Finally it was the last day of the trial. When the decision came, I couldn't hear the words. I saw mouths open and close. I looked at Mum. What was she thinking? I couldn't tell. The woman next to her was crying.

Then I heard the words.

♦

Sephy

It was two weeks after the trial. I was in the garden when Mother called me. 'Go to your room and put on your blue dress.'

That dress cost more than one thousand pounds. Why did she want me to wear it? It wasn't a special day or anyone's birthday.

'Where are we going?'

'Don't ask questions,' Mother said angrily. 'Go! And tell your sister to hurry.'

When we were ready, we went out to Dad's car. He was sitting in the back.

'Dad!' I ran to the car. I didn't see him very often these days.

'Sephy, get into the car,' he ordered. He didn't smile. Why wasn't he pleased to see me? We sat silently in the car, Mother, Minnie, Dad and I, not touching. Where were we going?

Just before six o'clock, our car stopped outside Hewmett Prison. There were lots of other cars there and people were walking in through the entrance. The guards let us into the prison. We followed them to some seats and we sat with a lot of other Crosses. The evening air was warm and uncomfortable. What was happening? I still didn't understand.

I looked around. The noughts were standing in silence, all dressed in black clothes. Some were crying. A few of them were looking angrily at the Crosses on the seats. They hated us.

'We are here today to watch the execution of Ryan Callum McGregor. He will hang by the neck until he is dead. Bring out the prisoner.'

Then I understood. A door opened and Callum's dad came out. I turned to Mother and Dad, but they were looking straight in front. Nobody spoke.

I saw Callum in the crowd of noughts. He was watching me and I was frightened by the look on his face. *I didn't know*, I said silently. *I promise, I didn't know. Please believe me, Callum.*

'Mother, I want to leave,' I whispered. I jumped to my feet. People were looking at me but I didn't mind. 'I can't stay here and watch this. I'm leaving.' I tried to push past the people next to me.

Mother stood up and hit me across my face. 'Sit down and don't say another word.'

I sat down and closed my eyes. I wanted to shut out the picture in front of me. But I couldn't keep my eyes closed. I opened them again and saw Callum. He was looking at me with hate in his eyes. I often saw that look on the faces of other noughts, but never on Callum's.

The prison guards put a black cloth over Callum's dad's head. It was nearly six o'clock, the time for the execution. Someone started to cry loudly, from the heart.

'Long live the Freedom Fighters!' Callum's dad shouted loudly.

♦

Callum

'WAIT! WAIT!' It was the voice of the prison governor. 'STOP THE EXECUTION!' he shouted.

What was happening?

The governor walked up to Dad and spoke to him. Then he turned to us. 'I am prison governor Giustini and I have just received new orders. Ryan Callum McGregor will stay in prison for the rest of his life. But there will be no hanging today.'

There was a lot of noise. The noughts were shouting and pushing forward. We wanted to reach Dad and get him out of there, but the guards took him back inside the prison.

The Crosses were leaving. I couldn't see Sephy. Where was she? Watching from somewhere? Enjoying the show? The Crosses were leaving quickly now, but the guards stopped and searched all the noughts at the gates. No Crosses were stopped.

I saw a man in front of me fall. People were getting hurt. There were angry screams and shouts. The noise excited me. I wanted to shout and kick too. I wanted to fight the Crosses. I wanted to kill them all.

Mum took hold of my arm. 'Callum!' she shouted. 'I want to see your dad. Let's go.' And she pulled me away from the crowd.

Two hours later we saw Dad. He looked terrible – old and small and pale. He saw us but he didn't smile. Mum put her arms around him and they stood silently for a long, long time.

Finally Mum spoke. 'How are you, Ryan?'

'How do you think?' Dad said angrily.

'I'm glad that you're alive.'

'I'm not. I was ready to die,' Dad said quietly. 'Do you think I want to spend the rest of my life in prison? Hanging is kinder. They'll keep me in here and kill me slowly.'

'Ryan – please don't lose hope.'

'Don't worry about me, Meggie,' Dad said. 'I'll find a way out of here.' He smiled a slow, frightening smile.

There were guards everywhere and high walls around the prison. He couldn't escape.

♦

Sephy

'Don't ever do that to me again!' I shouted. 'What were you and Dad thinking? Taking me to an execution? Are you both crazy?'

'Don't talk to me like that!' Mother had another drink. 'And

31

I didn't like it either.' She took hold of my arm. 'You don't know everything, Persephone. Ryan McGregor was my friend. Meggie was my friend too. I didn't want to watch his execution.'

'Why did you go then?' I shouted at her. 'You say they were your friends? How can you watch one of your friends hang?'

'I tried to help Ryan,' Mother whispered. 'I paid for their lawyer.'

'You paid for the lawyer?'

'Yes – but don't tell anyone.'

'So you felt guilty?' I shouted. 'You only ever think about yourself!'

I ran upstairs to my bedroom and lay on my bed. And then I cried – for Callum, for his dad, for that day, and for myself.

It was a long time before I heard the noise at the window. Somebody was throwing small stones at the glass. Callum …

He was in our garden. I opened the window.

'I need to see you,' he said softly. Then he climbed up the tree next to the window and into my room.

We stood in the middle of the room. He looked at me and I looked at him. I wanted to say sorry, for his dad, for everything. But the words in my head weren't good enough. It was better to say nothing.

'Is your father proud of himself?' Callum demanded. 'He ordered the prison governor to stop the execution. My father didn't kill anyone, but he'll stay in prison for the rest of his life. He'll never be free. That will make the Crosses happy.'

I didn't move or make a sound. Callum was hurting so much.

'I know your dad didn't do it. I'm so sorry.' I felt a tear run down the side of my face.

'I want to kill you and every other dagger that I meet. It frightens me how much I hate you,' he told me.

'I know,' I whispered. 'You've hated me since I called you a blanker.' I realised it as I said it.

'And you've hated me because I stayed away from you at school,' Callum said. His voice changed. 'So why are we still together? Why do I still think of you as ...'

'... your best friend? Because ... because I love you. And you love me, I think ...'

The cold, angry look returned to Callum's face. 'I don't believe in love. And a nought and a Cross can't be friends,' he said.

'Then why are you here?' I asked. I moved to the bed and sat down. After a minute, Callum sat down next to me. *What can I say to him?* I thought. *I want to say so much, but I can't find the right words.*

I turned to him and held out my arms. He moved slowly towards me and then he kissed me. We lay quietly on the bed.

'Callum,' I whispered. 'I'm sorry I sat at your table at school.' *And I'm sorry for a million other things, Callum. Sorry. Sorry.*

'Forget about it. I have,' he said softly, and he kissed me again.

Chapter 8 The Kidnap

'Ryan Callum McGregor, the Dundale Shopping Centre bomber, was killed this morning while he was trying to escape from Hewmett Prison. Four days ago, government ministers stopped his execution. His family refused to speak to our reporters.'

♦

Callum

I went into the café. This Friday was like every other Friday. The days were passing very slowly. They killed ... they murdered my dad in July. When he died, part of me died too.

I went to the beach a few times but I never stayed for long. Sephy was never there. The beach was part of my past.

When I received my food, I went to the darkest corner of the café. I ate slowly. I wasn't hungry, just bored. After Dad died, I was thrown out of school. I couldn't talk to Mum. Her husband and her daughter were dead, and her oldest son was missing …

'Hi, little brother.'

I looked up. Jude … Jude! I jumped up and put my arms around him.

'I've missed you,' I told him. 'Where were you?'

Jude looked around nervously. 'I was hiding.'

My smile disappeared. ' You … you know about Dad?'

'Oh yes, I know,' Jude said angrily. 'I know all about it. And now it's time for the Crosses to pay for his death.'

'What do you mean?'

Jude sat back in his chair. He looked nervously around the café again. 'What are you doing now?' he asked. 'Do you want to help us?'

'How?'

'I think you know, little brother. Just tell me one thing. Are you in or out?'

I understood his question. He wanted me to join the Freedom Fighters. Suddenly I felt calm. 'I'm in,' I said.

Jude stood up. 'We can change things. I have to go now. Go home and get some clothes. Someone will call you. You won't see Mum, or your friends, for a long time. I hope I can trust you.'

And then he quickly left the café.

The next day, Mum came into my room when I was putting clothes in my bag. 'Callum, what are you doing?'

'I'm going away, Mum. Somewhere where I can make a difference.'

Silence. Mum stood in the doorway watching me. 'I understand,' she said finally. 'When will you come back?'

'I don't know,' I answered honestly.

'Will you see your brother?'

'I don't know. Probably.'

'Tell him … Give him my love. And stay safe. Tell your brother to stay safe too.' She went downstairs.

I already had my orders. Go to the bus garage outside town and wait. I was joining the Freedom Fighters. Finally my life had a purpose.

At first I did small, unimportant jobs. But I quickly learned to be a soldier, and at the age of nineteen I was an officer.

There were four of us in my group: Pete, Morgan, Leila and me. Pete was the boss. He didn't say much but he smiled a lot. He always carried four knives – and he could kill with them. Morgan was good with computers, and Leila was our bomber.

I was the crazy one, the first person into danger and the last person out of it. I was a fighter. When I killed my first dagger, I felt nothing. Inside, I was a dead man.

I missed my mum. I sent money to her sometimes but I never saw her or my brother. Then two months after my nineteenth birthday, Jude came to us. 'I'm your new boss,' he said. He looked carefully at me. He still didn't quite trust me.

♦

Sephy

My mother sent me away to school for two and a half years. At first I didn't enjoy it. But after a few months I joined a group of Crosses who wanted to change the world. We wanted to make it a better place. We wanted noughts and Crosses to live together happily. I decided to be a lawyer when I was older. That gave a purpose to my future.

I often thought about Callum. I never heard from him after that one night we spent together. Did he think about me? Probably not.

And now I was nearly eighteen and I was home again. I hated the place. There were too many memories.

'Welcome home, Miss Sephy,' Sarah said. She looked around quickly. 'Someone left a message for you.'

She put an envelope in my hand. I knew the writing immediately. What did he want, after all this time? I began to read.

Dear Sephy

It's a long time since we met. Please meet me tonight at nine o'clock at the beach. It's very important. I will understand if you don't come. Two, almost three years is a long time.

C.

Why did he want to see me? Why was it important? Suddenly all my feelings for Callum came back. But did I really want to see him again? I had plans for my life, and we lived in different worlds.

Don't go, Sephy …

But just a short, ten-minute meeting …

Don't go …

♦

Callum

'Does everyone understand the plan?' Jude asked. 'Are you ready for this, little brother? Can we trust you?'

Everyone looked at me. 'Of course,' I said.

'This will make us famous,' said Morgan.

'And it will make the Freedom Fighters rich,' Jude said, smiling.

'What will we do if she doesn't come?' I asked.

'She got your message,' Jude said. 'She'll come. Follow orders and nothing will go wrong.'

♦

Sephy

I took off my shoes and walked a little way into the moonlit water. It was very quiet. I wanted to see Callum. I turned back towards the beach.

He was standing there. He looked so different, very tall and strong. He was a man, not a boy.

I stepped towards him and held out my arms. He didn't smile. 'Callum?' I said. Why wasn't he pleased to see me?

Callum stepped forward and kissed me, a short, cold kiss. Then he stepped away from me with sadness in his eyes and I saw them behind him. Four of them. Four noughts, walking towards us. Towards me. I looked at Callum, then I started to run, away from them, away from Callum. I ran to save my life.

I heard them shouting behind me. Run. Run. RUN. Don't look back … Don't think about Callum. Don't think about anything. JUST RUN. Run into the sea …

Somebody pulled me down onto the ground and hit me hard in the stomach. 'That's for my sister,' a voice said above my head. A man picked me up and held me tightly. He pulled me back across the beach. Rocks and stones cut my feet and my back. I was in pain and I started to cry. Then somebody put a bag over my head and the world went black.

Chapter 9 Held Prisoner

Callum

'We did it!' Jude shouted happily. 'We DID it!'

Yes, we did it. Persephone Hadley, Kamal Hadley's daughter, was our prisoner until Kamal agreed to our demands. We hid her in a place where nobody could find her.

'I'm proud of you, little brother,' Jude said.

I pushed him against the wall. 'Now do you trust me?' I said. 'I'm a friend of the Freedom Fighters, not the Crosses.'

'You did a good job,' he told me softly. 'Now we'll send a letter to her father. We need to prove that she's our prisoner.'

'How?' I asked.

'What do you suggest?' Jude asked. He was testing me again. Did I love the Fighters more than Sephy?

'I'll cut off some of her hair and film her with today's newspaper.'

'Is that enough?' Jude asked.

Another test. *Forget that our prisoner is Sephy*, I told myself. *She's just another Cross female ...*

'We need something of hers with her blood on it. I'll get it.' I picked up the camera and a sharp knife, and went to Sephy's prison cell.

♦

Sephy

Somebody unlocked the door and I sat up on my bed. My stomach, my neck – every part of my body hurt. The door opened. Callum ...

This was a new Callum, not my old friend. He stepped towards me and I moved away from him. Was that sadness in his eyes again? Then I saw the knife in his hand ...

I must not cry. I must not cry ...

His hands touched my head and he cut off some of my hair. Just my hair.

'I'm going to film you holding today's newspaper,' he said.

'No. I'm not going to help you.'

Two other noughts, a man and a woman, came into the room and stood behind Callum.

'Hold that paper or we'll break your arms,' the man said. I knew him. It was Jude, Callum's brother.

'I don't need your help,' Callum told them.

'I'm just watching, little brother.'

'I've come to see the daughter of the famous Kamal Hadley,' the woman said. Her voice was full of hate. I was a Cross, and the daughter of a government minister.

'Leila, go outside and guard the front door,' Jude told her.

She looked angrily at me and left the room.

'I want you to read out this message for your father,' Callum told me. He gave me a piece of paper and lifted up the camera. I looked quickly at the paper, then I threw it on the floor. 'Dad, don't give them any money,' I shouted.

Jude ran across the room and hit me hard across the face. 'You will do everything that we tell you. If you don't, we'll kill you. Do you understand?' He pushed me onto the bed. Then he walked out of the room and I was alone with Callum.

I wanted him to talk to me. I was a person, with a name and thoughts and feelings.

'Callum, I understand why you're angry. But this is wrong. You can't change the world by fighting ... There are other ways.'

'Be quiet,' he said. 'I'm not interested. Hold up the newspaper and read the words on this paper.' He picked up the camera again.

'Callum, please ...'

'READ IT!'

'Dad, the Freedom Fighters have kidnapped me. Follow their orders or I will die. They'll kill me if you go to the police. They're watching you. Please do what they say.'

When I finished, Callum took my T-shirt. He cut my finger with his knife and covered the T-shirt in my blood.

'Do you enjoy hurting me?' I asked, quickly pulling on my jacket. 'Jude wants to kill me. Does he hate me because I'm a Cross? Or because I'm Sephy Hadley? And you and I were friends. Have you forgotten that night ... ?'

'Two days later, you murdered my father,' Callum said angrily.

'I didn't want him to die,' I said. 'He was trying to escape.'

'You and the other Crosses killed him,' Callum shouted.

'And now one of you is going to kill *me*,' I whispered.

♦

Callum

Jude took the hair, the film and the T-shirt. He was pleased with the blood. 'Now I know you're one of us,' he said. 'Good work. Pete and I will take these. You guard Sephy Hadley. We'll be back here in the morning. The boss is sending one of his top men to join us. Look after him.'

That night, I couldn't sleep. I remembered Sephy's words. *One of you is going to kill me …*

Suddenly the door opened and Leila came in with a stranger. He was a tall man with long hair and expensive clothes. 'I'm Andrew Dorn,' he said. 'Assistant to the head of the Fighters. The boss thinks you've done well. Now I want to see the prisoner.'

I took him to the cell and opened the door. Sephy looked carefully at his face and then at his boots. I looked at his boots too. They were brown with very pointed toes. Unusual, but not special.

'If you're a good girl, we'll free you,' Andrew told her.

Sephy didn't speak. She was looking at him strangely.

I followed Andrew out. 'She must not leave this room alive,' he said quietly. 'Those are your orders.'

Jude and Pete came back and later that night we watched television. At seven o'clock, there was a news report. Kamal Hadley was following our orders.

'I am leaving the government for a short time for family reasons,' he told reporters. 'I do not want to say any more. Thank you.'

'Yes!' Jude said excitedly. 'He'll give us the money that we want. Then we'll make more demands. We'll tell him to free five Freedom Fighters from prison. Leila, you stay here with the girl. Pete, Morgan and I will make phone calls from different places in town, so the police won't find us. Callum, you'll pick up the money and leave the second list of demands.'

'Leila can get the money,' Andrew said. 'They won't notice a girl. Hadley knows Callum. Callum can stay here with Sephy.'

I wasn't happy, but I agreed.

'Let's go, people,' Andrew said. 'Be careful. The daggers are very clever.' He turned to me. 'If the police come, shoot the girl. Understand?'

'Yes.'

'Good.'

I didn't want to be there, near Sephy. I didn't want to see her face or hear her voice. She was still beautiful. And I still loved her.

Chapter 10 The Hidden Enemy

Sephy

I was lying on my back in my cell, holding my stomach. It was hurting where Jude hit me.

'What's wrong? Sephy, what's wrong?' Callum moved into the room and stood next to my bed.

'It's nothing. Go away.' I didn't look at him. I didn't want to cry. He was my enemy now. My Callum was dead.

I felt him sit down on the bed. Suddenly he put his hand on my stomach. I opened my eyes and looked at him.

'What are you doing?' I whispered.

'You're hurting.'

'And?'

'And I love you,' he said softly.

'Then free me. *Please …*'

Callum placed his fingers against my mouth. 'I always loved you. Do you hate me?'

Callum loved me …

'No,' I said, and tears ran down my face. 'But it's the wrong time and the wrong place for us.'

'There is no other time and place for us,' Callum said. And he kissed me softly.

This wasn't real. It was unnatural. It was against the law. I was dreaming. We were in a world where there were no noughts and Crosses. Just me and Callum ...

'Callum ... '

'I won't hurt you,' he said. 'I love you.'

I pulled him closer to me. It was true. There was no other time for us, only now. He touched my face, my hair. Then he lay down next to me. Nothing mattered – only this.

Much later, I sat up and pulled on my clothes. I couldn't stop crying. I was crying because there was no future for us.

'Sephy ...' Callum began. He looked so unhappy too. 'Sephy, please ...' He tried to put his arms around me. I pushed him away.

Then the door opened and Jude and Morgan ran into the cell. They stopped when they saw Callum and me on the bed. Callum jumped up, but it was too late ...

'What happened?' Callum asked Jude.

'*You* tell *us*,' Jude said angrily, looking from Callum to me. 'They caught Leila, and Pete is dead. There were police everywhere. Morgan and I were lucky to escape. Why is she crying?' He pointed at me.

Callum didn't speak but his face went red. Then a look of realisation passed across Jude's face.

'You stupid ... What have you done to her? They'll hang us all now.' Jude took hold of Callum's T-shirt. 'You stupid, stupid ... '

Suddenly they were fighting and they weren't looking at me. I ran to the open door. It was almost midnight, but the moon was full. I started to run towards the woods.

Run, Sephy. Run.

I ran through the trees, the moonlight bright around me. They mustn't catch me. Then something sharp cut my right foot and I screamed.

'Over there!' a voice shouted behind me, too close behind me.

'Persephone, I know you can hear me ...' It was Jude's voice.

'Come out now and we won't hurt you. I promise.'

Silence. After a few minutes, I heard his footsteps move away. I started to run again, then stopped. Callum stood in front of me, less than a metre away.

'Callum,' I whispered. He put a finger to his mouth.

'We have to find her,' another man shouted.

'I CAN SEE HER!' Callum shouted suddenly. 'She's running back towards the house.'

I heard them running, away from me, away from us. Callum stepped towards me and took my hands in his.

'When you reach the road, turn left.'

'Callum, we have to talk …'

'Just go, Sephy.' He turned away again.

'Callum …' And then I remembered. 'Wait. That man who came into my cell with you? He works for my father. I saw him, years ago, at our house.'

'Are you sure?' Callum asked.

'Yes. He works for Dad. He wore the same brown boots with the pointed toes. I know it was him.'

'Thanks.' He disappeared into the shadows.

I turned and ran.

Chapter 11 Family History

Callum

Jude, Morgan and I were hiding in a dirty little hotel, hundreds of kilometres from the house in the woods. We were watching Kamal Hadley on television.

'My daughter is home. The doctors say that she is very ill. The police will talk to her when she is awake. We were given information about her kidnappers and we caught one of them. Another was killed. No money was paid to them.'

Jude turned off the television and I told him about Andrew Dorn. At first he didn't believe me.

'Sephy lied to you! Andrew Dorn is the boss's assistant.'

'Only five people – and Andrew – knew our plans. One is dead. One was caught by the police. We three are here. That leaves Andrew. He wanted me to kill Sephy. He knew that she knew.'

Finally, Jude and Morgan believed me.

'If we stay together, the police will find us,' Jude said. 'We'll go to different places and meet again in six months, on Callum's birthday. And we won't say anything about Andrew Dorn. He's a friend of important people. Nobody will believe us.'

Morgan went out to get us some food.

'Andrew will try to kill us,' Jude said quietly. He suddenly looked very tired. 'Do you want to hear a joke, little brother? Sephy and her family believe that they're better than us. And they're not.'

'What are you talking about?' I asked.

'Mum's grandfather was a Cross. She told me when I joined the Freedom Fighters. There's Cross blood in our bodies. Mum didn't want me to fight them but I hate them all even more now. I don't know if I'll see you again. But listen to me, Callum. Stay away from Persephone Hadley. Or she'll destroy you.'

Four months later, I was working in a garage three hundred kilometres away from home. I had nothing: no family, no Freedom Fighters. Then I heard the news on the radio.

'Is Persephone Hadley, daughter of Kamal Hadley, pregnant? She has always refused to speak about her kidnap. We can only guess what the nought kidnappers did to her …'

♦

Sephy

I was sick every morning for five days.
God help me! What am I going to do?

44

Minnie was the first person to realise. 'You'll have to tell Mother,' she said.

'Are you crazy?' I shouted. 'I can't tell her – not yet. Please, Minnie, don't tell anyone.'

But Minnie couldn't keep a secret, so soon I was sitting in the family room with my parents.

'We're sending you to a small private hospital,' Dad said. 'By tomorrow evening you won't be pregnant and we can all forget about it. We'll go away together on holiday.'

'You want to kill my child?' I asked.

'You don't want to keep it, do you?' Mother said. 'A child of your kidnapper? I'll take you to the hospital.'

'I'm not going to the hospital tomorrow,' I said quietly. 'I'm keeping my baby.'

'No, you're not,' Dad said. 'Don't be silly.'

'It's my body and my baby and I'm keeping it.'

Callum will come to me. He's near here. I can feel him.

♦

Callum

It took me a day to return home. I went to Sephy's house and waited in the rose garden. Suddenly she was standing behind me.

'It's dangerous for you here,' she whispered.

'I wanted to come. Is it true?'

'Yes,' she said. Then she stepped forward and put her arms around me. I pulled her close. She was having a baby. *Our baby.* Suddenly I wasn't angry with the world any more. I touched her stomach. She was carrying our child. There were tears in my eyes.

'If it's a boy, I'll call him Ryan, like your dad,' Sephy said. 'If it's a girl, I'll call her Rose – *Callie* Rose.'

'Sephy ... ' I had to ask. 'That night ... why did you cry? Did I hurt you?'

'Of course not. I cried because I love you. I'll always love you. But you're a nought and I'm a Cross, and there's no place for us. People will always stand between us. That's why I cried. For everything that we'll never have.'

I loved her so much. 'Sephy, let's leave here. Let's go away and live together. Even for a short time … '

Suddenly lights came on around us.

'Callum, run. RUN!'

But I couldn't see. Then somebody hit me and knocked me to the ground. I heard Kamal Hadley's voice.

'I brought in more police to guard the house. I had an idea that the kidnappers were coming back for you.'

'You've got the wrong man,' Sephy shouted. 'Callum hasn't done anything wrong. He saved my life when I escaped from my prison cell. He's the father of my child and I love him.'

Kamal Hadley spoke quietly but angrily. 'If you love a blanker, you aren't my daughter. You *will* go to the hospital tomorrow. DO YOU HEAR ME?'

And I heard Sephy crying.

My trial came and went. One day I lay on the bed in my prison cell, reading the newspaper. One report interested me: *The Freedom Fighters have stopped all their activities while they search for an enemy spy in the group …*

'Good work, Jude,' I said to myself. 'You found a way to tell the boss about Andrew Dorn.' Was it Jude? Was he alive?

'Cal, you have a visitor,' Jack said. Jack was my Cross guard, but he was a kind man and we were friends.

Another man came in: Kamal Hadley. Why was he here? What did he want? Jack left and Kamal shut the door.

'I want to make an agreement with you,' he said. 'If you agree, you won't hang. You'll stay in prison for eight to ten years, then you'll be free. You'll still be a young man with your life in front of you.'

I looked at him carefully. He hated me, but he needed my help. 'What do you want me to do?'

'Tell everyone that you attacked my daughter. She doesn't really want this child. She won't keep it if you're not going to die.'

I sat down on the bed. I felt sick. He wanted me to choose between my life and my child's life.

'What's your problem?' I asked. 'Sephy and I having a child, or all mixed-race children?'

'My feelings are not important,' Kamal said. 'What's your answer?'

My life? Or my baby's? Oh Sephy, what should I do?

I stood up slowly. It was time to choose. I looked into Kamal Hadley's eyes and gave him my decision.

♦

Sephy

Dad came into my room. I looked at him without speaking.

'Callum McGregor is going to die,' he said. 'But if you end this pregnancy, I will stop the execution. It's not too late to end it. There are ways … You can choose to save Callum,' Dad said. Then he left the room.

I can kill our child and save Callum, I thought. Then I can work hard to free him from prison. When he comes out, we can be together again. We can have more children … But will we be able to live with the death of our first child? Callum's life or our baby's? Oh Callum, what should I do?

Suddenly I knew the answer. I knew.

♦

Callum

It is my last day on earth. Sephy tells everyone that I didn't attack her. But nobody listens. I'm a nought who loves a Cross. She is having my baby. To the judge, I'm guilty.

47

I am sitting with Jack, ten minutes before the hanging. I don't want to die.

'Don't you think the world will be a better place one day under a white government?' I ask him. 'We'll all have the same education and jobs. Then everyone will be able to make a success of their lives.'

'That's just a dream,' Jack replies. 'Do you really think that a nought government will be fairer? People are people. We make mistakes. We destroy things.'

I don't agree with him. I believe that the world can get better. But in the future. Not now, not for me.

'Your girl, Persephone Hadley, tried to get in here,' Jack says quietly. 'But the prison governor stopped her. He had orders … '

'Jack, will you help me?' I ask. 'Can you give this letter to Sephy? Put it in her hand? Promise me.'

'I promise,' Jack says.

I wanted to do so many things before I die. I wanted to see my mum again. Poor mum. Her husband and daughter are dead; her oldest son is missing, and I … And I wanted to talk to Sephy. Is she still carrying my baby, or did her parents find a way? We never had enough time together. I wanted to see her one more time.

I hear the door open. *I don't want to die …*

Governor Giustini is standing outside my cell.

Don't cry, Callum. Don't show your fear. Don't show them …

'Put your hands behind your back, Callum,' Jack says. There are tears in his eyes. 'You're doing well. Be strong. Not long now.'

They take me outside. It is a perfect evening, the sun shining in the sky. The world is so beautiful. A lot of people are waiting, more than at my father's hanging. Lots of Crosses want to watch the show.

I don't want to cry … I don't want to die …

'Forgive me, Callum,' Jack whispers.

I turn my head towards him. 'Don't be silly, Jack. You did

nothing wrong.'

'You did nothing wrong,' says Jack.

I smile at him. 'Thanks for saying that.'

I look at the crowds. Is Sephy here? And the child that I'll never see. Sephy …

Jack pulls a cloth over my head and suddenly everything is black. Tears run down my face, but nobody can see them now.

'I LOVE YOU, CALLUM …'

Wait …

'I LOVE YOU, CALLUM. AND OUR CHILD WILL LOVE YOU TOO. I LOVE YOU, CALLUM. I'LL ALWAYS LOVE YOU …'

I can hear her. She is there.

'I LOVE YOU TOO, SEPHY …' Can she hear me? 'I LOVE YOU, SEPHY. I LOVE YOU, SEPHY.'

Wait … Please wait … Just a minute longer.

'I LOVE YOU, CALLUM …'

'SEPHY, I …'

♦

BIRTHS

At midnight on 14 May, a beautiful daughter, Callie Rose, was born to Persephone Hadley.

Persephone wants people to know that Callie Rose will take the family name of her dead father – McGregor.

ACTIVITIES

Chapters 1–2

Before you read

1 Look at the Word List at the back of the book. Check the meanings of words that are new to you. Then use these words in the story below:

*lawyer   cell   freedom   kidnap   guilty   trial
confession   fingerprints*

> The man **a)** ..... . a woman and child and asked for
> £100,000. The police caught him and put him in a police
> **b)** ..... . They took his photograph and **c)** ..... . Then a
> **d)** ..... came to talk to the kidnapper. 'Yes, I'm **e)** .....,'
> the man said. 'I want to make a **f)** ..... .' At the man's **g)** .....,
> the judge sent him to prison for twenty years. 'I was stupid,'
> the criminal said. 'Now I've lost my **h)** ..... .'

2 *Noughts and Crosses*, the title of this book, is also the name of a game for two people.

   a Play the game a few times with another student.
   Student A: Place an X in one of the boxes.
   Student B: Place an O in another box.
   Continue placing Xs and then Os.
   The winner is the first person to have
   three Xs or three Os in a line.

   b Read the Introduction to the book. Why did Malorie Blackman use *Noughts* and *Crosses* as the title of the story?

3 What are these people called?

   a Callum's mother   ....

   b Callum's father   ....

   c Callum's brother   ....

   d Callum's sister   ....

   e Sephy's mother   ....

   f   Sephy's father   ....

   g Sephy's sister   ....

After you read

  4 Answer these questions.

    a Why does Mr Hadley hit his wife?

    b Why is Meggie's job so important to the McGregor family?

    c Who is older, Sephy or Callum?

    d Whose family has more money, Sephy's or Callum's?

    e Who control the country, the noughts or the Crosses?

    f Why, in this book, is the name noughts written with a small *n*?

    g What is unusual about Lynette?

  5 Work with another student. Talk about the McGregor and Hadley families.

    Student A: You are Sephy. Describe your family and your home. What is good about your life? What is bad about it?

    Student B: You are Callum. Describe your family and your home. How do you feel about your parents, brother and sister?

Chapters 3–4

Before you read

  6 Discuss these questions.

    a What will happen when Callum goes to Highcroft School? Will he be welcome there? Will he enjoy it?

    b Why will it be difficult for Callum and Sephy to be friends at school?

While you read

7 Are these sentences right (✓) or wrong (✗)?

    a Callum gets hurt during his first day at school   ......

    b Sephy hurts Callum without meaning to.   ......

    c The Cross teachers don't want nought pupils in Heathcroft School.   ......

    d The Freedom Fighters are a group of Crosses   ......

    e Noughts have pale skin.   ......

    f Sephy is attacked by some nought girls.   ......

    g Callum tries to visit Sephy.   ......

    h Lynette believes that she is a Cross.   ......

    i Years ago, she was attacked by noughts.   ......

    j Lynette's boyfriend was a nought.   ......

After you read

8 Complete these sentences.

    a When Sephy arrives at school, she ...

    b Callum is angry with Sephy because ...

    c If Callum talks to Sephy at school, she ...

    d When Callum hears about the attack on Sephy, he ...

    e When Jude hits Callum, their father ...

    f Three men attacked Lynette because ...

9 Imagine that you are Callum. You heard Sephy compare people in the crowd to 'blankers'. How do you feel towards her now? Did it make you angry? Do you still want to be her friend? Talk about your feelings.

Chapters 5–6

Before you read

10 Look at the titles of the next two chapters. What do you think is going to happen? Discuss these questions.

    a Chapter 5 *A Death in the Family*
       Who do you think is going to die?

    b Chapter 6 *The Bomb*
       What is a bomb used for? Who will place a bomb? What will happen?

While you read

11 Circle the correct answers.

    a Who tries to kill herself?

Mrs McGregor   Mrs Hadley   Minerva

b Who does Lynette leave a letter for?

Jude   Mr McGregor   Callum

c Who pushes Sephy?

Jude   Mr McGregor   Callum

d Where does Sephy go with her mother?

a café   a shopping centre   the beach

e How many people are killed by the bomb?

five   six   seven

f Who makes a confession about the bomb?

Jude   Mr McGregor   Callum

After you read

12 Who is speaking? Who to? What are they talking about?

a 'Did you really want to bring that child into our house?'

b 'She's lonely.'

c 'You're a weak man!'

d 'I'm afraid we have some bad news.'

e 'We don't want you here.'

f 'Y-you knew …'

g 'You *murdered* all those people …'

h 'I wanted to save Jude.'

13 Work with another student. Have this conversation (but talk quietly!).

Student A: You are Mrs McGregor. Ask your husband questions about the bomb at the shopping centre. Do you believe that he put it there? Why has he made a confession?

Student B: You are Mr McGregor. Answer your wife's questions. Explain why you made the confession.

Chapters 7–8

Before you read

14 Look at the titles of the next two chapters. What do you think will happen to these people?

a Mr McGregor

b Jude

c Callum

d Sephy

15 Put these sentences in the right order. Number them 1–8.

    a An unknown person pays the bills for Mr McGregor's lawyer. ......

    b Callum joins the Freedom Fighters. ......

    c Sephy and Callum meet at the beach. ......

    d Sephy and her family go to the execution. ......

    e The prison governor stops the execution. ......

    f Callum secretly visits Sephy in her house. ......

    g The court decides that Mr McGregor is guilty. ......

    h Sephy leaves home and goes away to school. ......

After you read

16 Which words are correct?

    a At the execution, the *Crosses/noughts* wear black clothes.

    b Ryan McGregor is *happy/angry* when the execution is stopped.

    c *Jasmine/Kamal* Hadley paid for Mr McGregor's lawyer.

    d There are *four/five* people in Callum's group of Freedom Fighters.

    e Sephy wants to help noughts by becoming a *doctor/lawyer*.

    f Callum sends a *package/message* to Sephy.

    g Sephy is kidnapped at *the beach/her house.*

17 Imagine that you are Sephy. Callum visited you in your house, then you didn't hear from him again. How did you feel? Were you angry with him? How did you feel when you received his message two and a half years later? Why did you go to the beach? Explain.

Chapters 9-11

Before you read

18 How do you think this story will end?

    a Will it end happily? Why (not)?

    b What will happen to these people?

      Callum   Sephy   Jude

While you read

19 Complete these sentences (a-j) with the endings (1-10) below.

    a Callum proves to Jude that ......

b Leila hates Sephy because ......

c A message is sent ......

d While the others phone ......

e Callum tells Sephy that ......

f Sephy escapes because ......

g Sephy tells Callum that ......

h Callum meets Sephy before ......

i Mr Hadley visits Callum to ......

j Sephy has to ......

    1) Callum helps her.

    2) make a terrible decision.

    3) make an agreement with him.

    4) Sephy is left alone with Callum.

    5) he goes to prison.

    6) he still loves her.

    7) Andrew Dorn works for her father

    8) she is a Cross.

    9) from Sephy to her father.

    10) he is a true Freedom Fighter.

After you read

20 Discuss why these are important in the story.

    a the brown plaster

    b fingerprints

    c Andrew Dorn's shoes

    d Meggie McGregor's grandfather

    e the name that Sephy gives to her baby

21 What lessons can we learn from the story of *Noughts and Crosses*?

Writing

22 Go to www.marjorieblackman.co.uk on the Internet. Find three interesting pieces of information about the writer of *Noughts and Crosses* and her work. Then tell other students what you have learnt.

23 Describe your first day at a new school. What happened when you arrived? Did you enjoy your lessons? Were the teachers and other students friendly? What problems did you have?

24 You are a teacher at Heathcroft School. Nought pupils are coming to your school for the first time. Write ten rules for them that are different to the rules for Cross students.

25 You are Jude, at the time when you are still living at home. Write about your family and your feelings for them. Explain why you are always angry with Callum and Lynette. Describe your plans for the future. How will you help the noughts fight the Crosses? Why?

26 Imagine that you are Ryan McGregor. Write your 'confession' to the police about the shopping centre bomb.

27 Imagine that you are a Cross reporter at the execution of Ryan McGregor. Write a report for your newspaper. Describe what you see and hear. What happens to the prisoner?

28 You are Callum and you now belong to the Freedom Fighters, but before the kidnap. Write a secret letter to your mother. Explain why you joined the Fighters. Describe your life and the other people in your group.

29 You are a police officer. You are going to question Callum after he is caught at Sephy's house. Write a list of ten questions for him about the kidnap and the Freedom Fighters.

30 You are Callum. It is the night before your execution. Write a letter to Sephy and your unborn child. Describe your feelings for them. What do you hope will happen to them in the future?

31 Write a telephone conversation between Sephy and Minerva after the end of the story. (Sephy wants to tell Minerva about her baby. How does Minerva feel about this child and about Callum's death?)

32 Write about this book for your friends. Introduce the story. What did you learn about the world of the noughts and Crosses? Do you think this is an important book? Why (not)?

Answers for the Activities in this book are available from the Pearson English Readers website. A free Activity Worksheet is also available from the website. Activity worksheets are part of the Pearson English Readers Teacher Support Programme, which also includes Progress tests and Graded Reader Guidelines. For more information, please visit: www.pearsonenglishreaders.com

WORD LIST

bomb (n/v) something that can kill many people. A large *bomb* in a building will destroy that building, with a loud noise.

cell (n) a small room where prisoners are kept

confession (n) a statement that you have done something wrong

control (v) to make sure that people do things. If you *control* people, you have this ability.

demand (n/v) a strong request for something that, in your opinion, should be given

educate (v) to teach someone in a school or college

execution (n) the act of killing someone, usually to punish them for a crime

fingerprint (n) the shapes made by the lines in the skin on the end of your finger. Each person leaves a different *fingerprint* when they touch something.

freedom (n) the state of being free

guilty (adj) having done something criminal

hang (v) to kill someone by dropping them from a great height with a strong line around their neck

kidnap (n/v) the crime of taking someone, usually before asking for money for their return

lawyer (n) someone who has studied the law. He or she tells people about it and can speak for them in court.

minister (n) someone with an important position in the government

nought (n) the number zero (0)

plaster (n) a piece of special cloth for covering a cut on a person's skin

pregnant (adj) carrying an unborn baby inside your body. This is a state of **pregnancy**.

trial (n) a time, in a courtroom, when a possible criminal is in front of a judge. People are questioned and a decision about the man or woman is then made.

trust (v) to believe that someone is honest

whisper (v) to say something very quietly. You *whisper* when you don't want other people to hear you.